Groom Your Room

Terrific Touches to Brighten Your Bedroom!

PLEASANT COMPANY PUBLICATIONS™

Published by Pleasant Company Publications
© Copyright 1997 by Pleasant Company

Printed in the United States of America.
98 99 00 WCR 10 9 8 7 6 5 4

American Girl Library® is a trademark of Pleasant Company.

Editorial Development: Trula Magruder, Michelle Watkins
Art Direction: Kym Abrams
Design: Amy Nathan, Kate Evans
Styling: Lee Ann Perry, Deborah Pike, Pamela Swartchild, Anne Lepley Wilkins
Photography: Michael Walker, Fritz Geiger, Tosca Radigonda, Paul Tryba, Alan Shortall

All the instructions in this book have been tested by children and adults. Results from their testing were incorporated into this book. Nonetheless, all recommendations and suggestions are made without any guarantees on the part of Pleasant Company Publications. Because of differing tools, ingredients, conditions, and individual skills, the publisher disclaims liability for any injuries, losses, or other damages that may result from using the information in this book.

Portions of this book have previously been published in *American Girl*® magazine.

Library of Congress Cataloging-in-Publication Data
Groom your room : terrific touches to brighten your bedroom!
p. cm. "American girl library (Middleton,Wis.)."
Summary: Offers ideas and advice that allow girls to create bedrooms that suit their personalities and lifestyles.
ISBN 1-56247-531-2
1. Handicraft—Juvenile literature. 2. Bedrooms—Juvenile literature. 3. Children's rooms—Juvenile literature. 4. Interior decoration—Juvenile literature.
[1. Interior decoration. 2. Bedrooms. 3. Handicraft.]
I. American girl (Middleton, Wis.)
TT171.G69   1997
745.5—dc21   97—20288   CIP   AC

Dear American Girl,

I would like to know how to make over my room without spending a lot of money, and by making or decorating some of the things myself. Please help me!

Sincerely,
Nancy ReNae Kelso
Arizona

Inside these pages you'll find **fresh,** fun ways to groom your room without a lot of money or time. Looking for a major **makeover?** We've got ideas for everything from light switches to lampshades. Need some quick **decorating tips?** They're in here. Can't find the top of your desk? Try our clever ways to **organize** clutter. Decorate what's old, display what's new, and discover your **style.** Best of all, you can do it **yourself!**

Your friends at *American Girl*

What do I do with this?

pages 15, 20, 21

pages 7, 29, 32, 33, 37

pages 21, 30, 31, 33, 34

pages 10, 11

pages 21, 29

page 20

page 18

pages 16, 33, 45

page 21

pages 42, 43, 44, 46

pages 7, 22, 23, 26, 28, 29

pages 14, 19, 20, 22

Is your room filled by the items we show? Then turn to the pages listed below. Organize and decorate just like a pro!

pages 19, 22, 25

pages 33, 35, 37, 46

pages 20, 22, 31, 34, 35, 45, 46

pages 14, 31

pages 15, 17, 20, 24, 25, 45

pages 12, 13, 45, 46

page 19

pages 32, 37, 45

pages 7, 19, 22, 28

pages 16, 20, 29

pages 22, 24, 28

pages 38, 39, 40

A Clean Sweep!

Before you begin any project, clean up and clear the clutter so you know just what you're working with. These tips can make a clean sweep easier!

Attack the Big Mess

First make your bed, throw dirty clothes into a hamper, stack your books and magazines onto bookshelves. See? It's looking better already!

Make Vacuuming a Game

Here are the rules: Once the vacuum touches an area of carpet, you can't touch it again with your feet. Start in the corner farthest from the door, and make your way out of the room.

Play Music

Slip on a portable stereo or turn up the music to help get you in the mood!

Collect the Small Stuff

Wearing a fanny pack while you clean can save time. Use the fanny pack to hold little stuff until you're ready to put everything away.

Sort Through Papers

Toss the school papers you don't need, and find a place to store the ones you do. Old backpacks and suitcases make great storage cases, and they slip under beds.

Make a Promise

Put things away when you're through with them. It will make cleaning up a whole lot easier next time!

Wipe Out Dust Bunnies

Slip a sock onto your hand, spray it with furniture polish, and shine on! Slide a sock onto a yardstick and fasten it with a rubber band for hard-to-reach places—under beds, on overhead lights, and along ceiling corners.

Getting Started

Check out these helpful hints before you start any room improvements!

Very Important!

Be sure to get an adult's permission before you begin your project. Adults will want to know exactly what you plan on doing—especially if you want to make some big changes like painting furniture or putting nails into a wall!

This symbol means you'll need special help from an adult, usually for safety reasons. Of course, always follow your family rules when using hot appliances or sharp tools. Be sure to read carefully all instructions and warnings for materials like paints, dyes, and glues.

Directions

Before starting any project, carefully read through all the directions and the list of supplies. Make sure you have everything you need, you understand what to do, and you have enough time to finish the project.

Ready to Work

Pick a well-lighted place that's out of reach of pets and younger children. Cover your work surface with newspaper or a plastic tablecloth. Tie back your hair, roll up your sleeves, and wear a smock, an apron, or old clothes.

Materials

You probably have most of the materials you'll need right at home. If not, try substituting the materials with items you do have. You may need to call craft or fabric stores to see if they have what you need and how much the materials cost. Start saving ribbons, buttons, fabric scraps, and other useful items in a special arts-and-crafts box so you'll always have materials on hand.

Using Paint

Fabric paint: Always wash, dry, and iron fabric like sheets and pillowcases before painting on them, even if they're brand new. After the paint dries completely, cover the painted area with a cloth and iron it. This seals in the color so it won't come out when you wash it. Always have an adult help you with any ironing.

Acrylic paint: A foam brush works well for applying acrylic paints. Note: some items may require 2 coats.

Spray paint: If you have small hands, spray cans may be awkward to hold. If so, ask a parent to help. Use spray paints outside. Spread lots of newspaper beneath the item to be painted. Always aim the nozzle at the item before spraying!

Working with Fabric Glue

Always use a high-quality fabric glue. If working with a washable item, use a fabric glue that can be washed, like Aleene's OK to Wash-It. For best results, start at the center of the item and work to the edge using a 1-inch-wide foam brush. Read the glue bottle for washability. Generally, wash in cold water on the delicate cycle, and dry on gentle.

Switched-On Style

Pretty Paper

Create pretty paper patterns by gluing bits of brightly colored paper onto your switch plate.

Silk Flowers

Make a bouquet by gluing silk flowers onto your switch plate. Glue on ribbon stems, and paint a bug, too!

First, ask an adult to remove your switch plate from the wall. Then light up your switch plate—and your room—with style!

Art Supplies

Use decals, stickers, paint pens, or permanent markers to transform your switch plate into a work of art.

Ribbons and Rickrack

Glue on ribbon and some rickrack, too, for a bright, bold look.

Light It Up!

A plain lampshade is the perfect place to let your creativity shine through!

Bold Buttons

Use craft glue to attach big buttons evenly around the base of the lampshade. Glue smaller buttons in an arc around each big button. Finish off by gluing more small buttons around the top of the lampshade. Let dry overnight.

Daisy Crazy

Here's a project to make your room bloom! Buy a bunch of silk daisies. Cut the flowers off at their bases. Glue them onto the lampshade or the pull-chain with craft glue. Let dry overnight.

Star Shine

Use craft glue to apply appliqués to your lampshade in pretty patterns. Let dry overnight.

Ribbons and Beads

Cut about 20 lengths of ribbon, each about 2 inches longer than the height of the shade. Glue the end of each ribbon so it's flush with the top of the shade. String a bead onto the end of each ribbon, and knot the ribbon underneath so the bead hangs just below the bottom of the shade. Snip off the extra ribbon or let it hang.

Rickrack Rainbow

Put a thin line of craft glue around the top edge of the lampshade. Wrap the rickrack around the shade, pressing it on to the glue as it winds around. Cut the rickrack when you've made a full circle. Repeat with another piece of rickrack on the bottom of the shade. For the middle piece, first put the glue onto the rickrack, then press the rickrack into place.

13

Tie On Your Style!

Go Bandannas!

Slip a folded bandanna behind the curtain, and tie 2 simple knots. If you're having fun, don't stop at 1! Go for more—try 2, 3, or 4!

Easy Elegance

Make a pretty point of interest with pearls! Wrap the pearls around the curtain the way you'd wrap a rubber band around a ponytail. Carefully tie a knot with the dangling end.

Turn a plain curtain into a canvas of creativity with tiebacks. Wrap with a ribbon or bind with a belt—just tie on your style!

Flower Power

Hair accessories can tie up more than hair! Twist the band around the curtain, then center the decoration. Frame a window with flowers, or try other fun accessories!

Wrap On a Rope

Jump ropes aren't just for recess! Wrap a rope around your curtains, tie a knot, and drape the handles in front. Casual and cute!

Hold Everything!

Dress up your dresser top and store all sorts of little stuff in these cool, colorful tin cans and flowerpots.

Painted Cans

You will need:

- Tin can
- Medium-grade sandpaper
- Spray paint
- Office labels

1 Remove the label from the can and wash it in the dishwasher. Be careful of sharp edges. Sand the outside of the can with sandpaper to help the paint hold. Wipe off the can and let dry.

2 Go outside and spray-paint the inside and the outside of the can, making sure to cover the top rim. Let dry.

3 Decorate the can with brightly colored office labels or tape.

Petal Power

Crisscross 4 strips of colored tape onto the side of the pot. Stick a round office label in the center.

Fruit Fresh!

To make this watermelon, paint the inside of the pot pink. Paint the outside rim green. Let dry overnight. Cut out seed shapes from black tape and stick them along the inside rim.

Show
It O

Give

top rim. Let d
minutes. Paint a second coat if needed.

3 Decorate with office labels and colored tape. You can also glue on colored paper.

Off!

e a special
ollection its own
place to shine!

Sitting Pretty

Is a jumble of dolls gathering dust in your closet? A kiddie chair, a small cradle, or an old bassinet can be the perfect place to display your cuddly collection. Keep them dust-free with an occasional blast from a blow-dryer!

Wall of Fame

Hang a favorite sports jersey on a wooden dowel. Tie the ends of a long ribbon onto the ends of the dowel and hang it from a hook on your wall. Here's another winning idea: attach adhesive-backed hooks to the back of the door, and hang your colorful caps!

Bow Tied

Dancing shoes can make a dazzling display. First, tie the toe shoe ribbons together. Then tie them to a great big bow made from tulle, a net-like material you can find in fabric stores. Finally, hang them from a hook on your wall.

Perfect Perch

A three-tiered vegetable bin found in the kitchen can go to work in your room, too. Hang it from a hook on your ceiling, and presto, it's a Beanie Baby bin!

Put It Away!

Clear the clutter with space-saving devices made from everyday items like jars, cardboard boxes, crates—even a shoe holder!

Stock a Box

Put posters and precious artwork in a place all their own. Store rolled art in a divided cardboard box to prevent creases and wrinkles. Label the box so you'll know what's inside.

Clear It Up!

Use a shoe holder to store items that don't seem to have a home anywhere else. A see-through holder will help you find things in a jiffy!

Reach for the Jars!

Make your odds 'n' ends easy to reach with this great storage idea. Remove jar lids and paint them. After the paint dries, hammer a nail through the center of each lid to make a hole. Put a screw into each hole and screw the lid into the underside of a shelf. Fill the jars and attach them to the shelf with a twist of the wrist!

Cool Crates

Keep balls, bats, ice skates, and other sports gear from cluttering your closet floor by storing them in colorful milk crates. Stack them in a rainbow of colors, or use one for everything!

21

String Your Curtain Rings

String together shower curtain rings, then hang the string from your closet rod. Now slip ribbons, belts, or purses onto the rings.

Hang It Up

Drawers stuffed full? Hang jeans and sweatshirts in the closet. They get less wrinkled this way, too.

One-of-a-Kind

To save space, hang or fold one-of-a-kind items together: shirts, sweaters, jeans, etc. Also, keep the clothes you wear the most in the front of the closet, and hang other items toward the back.

Inside Guide

See-through bins let you see what's stored. Clearly label boxes that you can't see into.

Less Mess

Less stuff means less mess. Get rid of items you no longer use or wear. Sort these into 3 piles: a giveaway pile, a storage pile, and a garbage pile. Note: check with your parents before tossing out anything.

Dunk It In!

Score neater floors by dunking dirty laundry into a hamper or bin.

Shoe Stack

Stack shoes on a shelf to keep them organized and to help prevent scuff marks. Fit boots or everyday shoes onto higher shelves for easy reach.

Closet Control

Does your closet look like the lost-and-found? Organize clutter with these quick tips, and discover how much space you'll find!

Heads Up!

To keep track of hats, caps, bows, and barrettes, try these four easy tips.

Band Stand

Stop sifting through drawers in search of that perfect headband! Instead, try this trick: Cover a roll of paper towels with a piece of felt that's about 22 by 25 inches. Gather the extra felt at each end, and tie it with ribbon. Headbands will slip off and on easily and be right at hand when you need them!

Bunch Your Scrunchies

Keep scrunchies handy by slipping them onto a hanger with a removable cardboard bottom. To decorate, wrap wire with green florist tape, adding silk flowers as you wrap. Now hang it up!

Hat Trick

To create this clever cap rack, paint 3 clothespins and a yardstick. Let dry, then glue the clothespins to the yardstick. Tack the yardstick to a wall, and hang your hats high!

Barrette Set

Try this blue-ribbon idea! Cut a length of wide ribbon. Lay a narrow ribbon on top. Tie the ribbons together at one end. To stop barrettes from slipping, tie knots along the top ribbon.

Dressy Drawers

Your dresser will shine with style—inside and outside—with these top-drawer ideas!

It's a Wrap!

To make a simple drawer liner, measure the inside of your drawer, then cut a sheet of wrapping paper to fit.

All the Same

Keep your drawers organized by folding similar items in the same way. To fold socks, lay one sock on top of the other. Now roll them together from the toes out.

Sock Sachet

This idea makes scents! Sweeten up the smell of your sock drawer with a home-made sachet of potpourri. Mix pieces of cinnamon sticks, vanilla candles, eucalyptus leaves, and dried flowers. Slip the mix into a sock. Tie the sock with a pretty ribbon and drop it in your drawer!

Blue Sky

1 Trace the cloud pattern on page 47. Cut out the traced cloud, then place the cutout on the drawer and draw around it lightly with a pencil. Draw an outline of the sun's rays, too.

2 Paint the knob and the sun's rays with yellow paint. Paint 2 coats.

3 To make the clouds, pour white paint into a dish. Dip the sponge into the paint, then dab it onto newspaper to remove excess paint. Dab paint into the center of the cloud until you've filled in the outline. Let dry. Wipe off pencil lines with a damp cloth.

Flower Field

1 With the pencil, make light dots on each drawer where you want the flowers to be.

2 Trace the flower pattern on page 47 and cut it out. Center the cutout over each dot. With a pencil, lightly trace the flower's outline.

3 Paint the flowers. Let them dry, then paint the centers of the flowers. Dry overnight. Wipe off pencil lines with a damp cloth.

m for Two

make sharing a room half the hassle—or twice as nice!

lor Code

olor is a quick way to tell her stuff from yours—and whose stuff goes where! Each of you choose a color, and mark your spots. Get different-colored laundry baskets and hangers. Attach different-colored drawer pulls to your dresser.

Create Space

In a tight spot? Collapsible furniture, like card tables and TV trays, can come in handy when you're working on projects, doing jigsaw puzzles, or playing board games. After you're through, simply fold up the furniture and put it away.

Coordinate

If you want a teal comforter but your sister loves the pink one, don't fret. You can both have your way. Mix and match those colors on pieces you share—like rugs, curtains, lampshades, or throw pillows.

Control Clutter

Use an old backpack or suitcase to hold old papers, sports gear, or more. Label yours with a luggage tag!

★ Sisters' Constitution ★

I promise I won't:
★ play the radio if my sister is studying.
★ leave the dresser drawers open.

I promise I will:
★ always knock if the door is closed.
★ ask before I wear my sister's clothes.
★ keep my side of the room clean. Kristen Lisa

Compromise

If you and your sister can't agree on room rules, ask your mom to help the two of you create a "Sisters' Constitution"—a list of promises you agree to keep. Then both of you sign the paper and hang it in your room.

Get on Board!

Show off fancy fun-tacks on a bright new bulletin board.

Fun-tacks

1 Put a dot of Elmer's glue on the head of a thumbtack. Just a dab will hold most objects.

2 Press an object onto the tack, and hold for a few seconds. Let dry with tack head down.

Cheerful

Bored with your board? Brighten tacks with buttons, beads, plastics, and playthings!

Dainty

For a soft touch, glue on tiny appliqués, silk flowers, and pretty pom-poms!

Jolly

Use large or small colored tacks, then show off style with a shower of stickers.

Natural

Glue on shells, stones, or feathers. Go nutty with nature!

Flashy

Let your board shine with rhinestones. Or try glitter for a splash of flash!

Bulletin Board

With a thick piece of cardboard and a pretty piece of cloth, you can make your own bulletin board.

1 Cut fabric so it's 2 inches wider than the cardboard.

2 Center the cardboard on the back side of the fabric. Wrap the fabric over the edges and glue into place.

3 Wrap ribbons around the corners and bottom, and glue them onto the back of the cardboard.

Desk Set

Do supplies and schoolwork rule your work space? Control the paper flow with these simple, inexpensive desk mates!

Stamp Collector

Snatch up an empty matchbox to store your stamps. Glue used stamps onto the outside of your box to give it that well-traveled look!

Box It Up!

Keep your magazines handy by storing them in a cereal box on your desk. Just cut the box diagonally on both sides. Cover it with wrapping paper or contact paper.

Hit the Slot

Nab an old napkin holder to use as a desk organizer. No need to decorate it—just slip stationery or schoolwork into the slot.

My Mailbox

Make your desk letter-perfect with an old mailbox. To give the box a new look, paint it your favorite color and paint on your name. Stuff homework inside. When you need a paper for class, put up the red flag as a reminder!

Bands Together

Glass jars can do triple duty on your desk! Decorate jars with rubber bands to keep bands tidy. Store coins and other small items in the jars. And tuck notes between the bands to remind you of upcoming events.

Field trip Tuesday

Frame by Frame

Whether hanging on a wall or sitting on your desk, these frames will add a pretty point of interest to your room.

On Tack

Give plain frames terrific texture with colorful thumbtacks! Tacks work great with paper frames—like precut picture mats or frames cut from cardboard. If tacks won't insert completely, try the following steps:

1 Lay down a thick stack of newspapers. Press tacks partway into the frame.

2 Lay felt or a soft cloth over the tack and tap it lightly with a hammer.

3 If tack pins stick through the back, cut out more cardboard or a piece of foam core, available at frame shops or art supply stores. Glue it to the back of the frame.

Pencil Power

You'll want to sharpen a pencil on this idea—12 pencils, to be exact! Try mixing 2 colors, 3 colors, or filling the frame with a rainbow of color.

1 Sharpen both ends of each pencil until you have 4 long ones, 4 medium ones, and 4 small ones.

2 Spread craft glue onto the frame and place pencils on the frame as shown below. Let glue dry.

Chalk One Up!

Use chalkboard paint to turn a plain frame into an easel of expression. If you get tired of the look, simply erase it and start again.

1 Spread out newspapers. If your frame has glass, remove it. Lay the frame onto the newspapers.

2 For this step, you will need an adult to help or an adult's permission. Spray the frame with chalkboard paint, following the directions on the can. Let dry. Replace glass. Use chalk to draw designs or write messages!

Brick Tricks

Stick bricks all over your room for a fun fix of color. Stand them, stack them, or fill them with flowers!

Window Box

Bring the outside in all year round! First, find 4 bricks with 3 or more holes in their sides.

1 Brush bricks with a paintbrush to remove some of the grit. Attach strips of masking tape along the edge of each brick. Press the tape tightly to the brick's surface.

2 Paint stripes with a paintbrush or foam brush and acrylic paint. Let the bricks dry overnight.

3 Remove the tape. Stack the bricks together on your windowsill and fill with silk flowers.

Bookends

Keep your books in place with these heavy-duty bookends.

1 To make the star pattern, trace the star shape from page 47 onto tracing paper. Tape the tracing paper onto heavy paper, then trace and cut out about 10 stars.

2 Brush off bricks with a paintbrush to remove any grit. Stick the paper stars down with rubber cement.

3 Spray-paint the bricks outside. You'll need 2 coats of paint. Let dry 1 hour between coats. When the second coat is dry, peel off the stars. To keep bricks from scratching your furniture, glue felt to their bottoms.

Art Kit

Find some bricks with holes running through their sides. The holes are perfect for holding scissors, pencils, markers, and crayons. Stack 2 bricks behind the first one to make a double-decker art stand!

To decorate, add a few drops of water to acrylic paint, and flick the paint onto the bricks with a paintbrush. This is messy, so work outside, use lots of newspaper, and wear old clothes.

Pillow Talk

Perk up your pillows with these pretty patterns.

Ribbon Stripe

Cut 3 pieces of ribbon the length of the edge of a pillowcase. Spread a line of fabric glue along the back of the ribbon. Press it down onto a washed pillowcase. Repeat with the other 2 pieces of ribbon. Let dry overnight.

Painted Polka Dots

With a pencil, lightly trace circles onto one side of a plain, washed pillowcase. Then stuff a plastic bag into the pillow-case. This will keep the fabric paint from soaking through as you fill in the circles with a paintbrush. Keep the plastic bag in the pillowcase as it dries overnight.

Cozy
Coverlet

Make this beautiful spread to add color and comfort to your bed!

polar fleece provided by: Malden Mills, Room 1408, 4.00 Fr. Ave. New York, New York 10123

YOU WILL NEED

- 1¼ yards polar fleece for base
- Pinking shears
- Tracing paper
- Pencil
- Scissors
- Straight pins
- ¼ yard polar fleece pieces to make 9 big flowers and 4 small flowers
- ¼ yard green polar fleece to make 16 leaves
- Fabric glue that can be washed
- Paper cup
- Cardboard
- 1-inch-wide foam paintbrush
- 13 acrylic pom-poms

1 With the pinking shears, cut the top border of the coverlet base to give it a decorative edge.

2 Flowers: Trace the patterns on page 48 onto tracing paper and cut them out. Pin the paper flowers to the polar fleece pieces and cut around them with scissors, making 9 big flowers and 4 smaller ones.

3 Leaves: Using the leaf pattern on page 48, follow the same process as in Step 2. Use the pinking shears to cut 16 leaves from the green polar fleece.

4 Arrange the flowers and leaves before gluing to make sure you like the pattern.

5 Put the fabric glue into the cup. Place a flower onto the cardboard. With the paintbrush, apply an even layer of fabric glue onto the back of each petal. Start at the center and spread glue all the way out to the edges. Press each flower firmly into place onto the coverlet base. Do not rub.

6 Use the brush to put a generous dab of fabric glue onto each pom-pom. Press each pom-pom firmly onto the center of each flower. Let dry overnight.

Care tip: Wash in cold water on the delicate cycle and dry on the gentle cycle.

Fun Furniture

Show off your flair with one of these charming chairs!

Night Sky

Glow-in-the-dark paint makes a plain chair shine.

1 Trace the 3 star patterns on page 47 onto tracing paper, and cut them out. With the pencil, lightly trace the stars onto the chair.

2 Cover your work area with newspapers. Carefully fill in the stars with the yellow paint. Let dry overnight.

3 Repaint the stars with glow-in-the-dark paint. Let dry. Wipe off pencil outlines with the damp rag.

Light Bright

A slat- or rod-back chair makes a perfect rainbow.

1 Spread newspapers over your work area. Using the 1-inch brush, paint each chair rod or slat a different color. Be sure to rinse the brush between colors. Let the chair dry overnight.

2 Use painters' tape, available at hardware stores, to cover the ends of each painted rod. Using the wider 2-inch brush, paint the chair seat yellow and the top edge of the chair blue. Let dry, then slowly remove the tape so you don't peel off the paint.

3 Using the 2-inch brush again, paint the legs different colors. Let dry.

An adult to help you or an adult's permission
- Tape measure
- Scissors
- Heavy-duty mounting tape, sold at hardware stores. This 2-sided tape has a peel-off backing on one side.
- Chair
- Tulle. To measure the width, wrap a tape measure around the seat edge, then multiply by 3. To measure the length, hold the tape measure from the top of the seat to 2 inches above the floor, then multiply by 2.
- Fabric glue
- Pink satin ribbon about 1 to 2 inches wide

Ballet Beauty

This chair is pretty in pink!

1 Measure and cut the mounting tape to fit around the seat edge. Stick the tape around the seat edge, but don't remove the peel-off backing yet.

2 To attach the tulle to the chair, remove the peel-off backing from the tape. Fold the tulle in half. Firmly press the folded edge of the tulle onto the tape, gathering it into 1-inch pleats as you go.

3 Measure the ribbon so there's enough to wrap around the seat edge and overlap about an inch. Spread a thick line of fabric glue along the tulle-pleated edge. Starting in back, carefully glue the ribbon around the seat. As an option, you can leave about 18 inches of ribbon on both ends and tie a bow in back.

Create Your Own Style

To give your room a designer's scheme, choose color, pattern, texture, or theme.

Daisy Crazy

Surround yourself with things you love and your room will magically come together. If you love daisies, make a daisy lampshade, stick fresh daisies in a jar, or paint a can with daisy-yellow spots.

A Soft Touch

Accent pieces will pull together furniture that doesn't match. For instance, if you prefer soft colors, try adding softer accents, such as a ribbon shade, a pink frame, or pastel pots.

Quick Color

Add quick splashes of color to cheer up any room. Go for bold buttons on a lampshade, bright touches on a frame—even a cheerful knickknack, like this perky pig!

Star Quality

A repeating pattern will bring balance and harmony to a room. Paint stars on bricks, glue stars to a shade, or tie up your curtains with a star-covered scarf.

The Great Outdoors

Coordinate furniture and accent pieces with a theme. Try this one: bring the outdoors inside! Paint clouds on a dresser or a rainbow on a chair, glue rainbow rickrack to a lampshade, and display a rainbow frame.

Patterns

Trace these patterns, following the directions for each project.

Bookends, **page 37**

Blue Sky, **page 27**

Flower Field, **page 27**

Night Sky, **page 42**

Cozy Coverlet, page 41

Follow this pattern to make the coverlet.